Mae Douglas Durell Frazar

Ten Days in Switzerland

Mae Douglas Durell Frazar

Ten Days in Switzerland

ISBN/EAN: 9783337155636

Printed in Europe, USA, Canada, Australia, Japan

Cover: Foto ©Andreas Hilbeck / pixelio.de

More available books at **www.hansebooks.com**

TEN DAYS

IN

SWITZERLAND

BY MRS. M. D. FRAZAR,

BOSTON, MASS.

BOSTON:
J. A. CUMMINGS PRINTING CO , 252 WASHINGTON STREET.
1891.

TEN DAYS IN SWITZERLAND.

CHAPTER I.

TEN DAYS IN THE COUNTRY OF BEAUTIFUL SCENERY—
THE GRAVE OF KEMBLE—GIBBON'S GARDEN—
GLIMPSES OF MONT BLANC—GENEVA—
THE HOME OF CALVIN.

After busy, feverish days of sightseeing in London and Paris, the atmosphere of Switzerland is like a benediction.

Leaving Paris in the morning, an all-day ride is made through France by the way of Dijon, and one arrives at night, after dark, at Lausanne. The carriage that takes us to our hotel winds up and up the hilly roads till we reach a sort of main street, and we begin to think we have arrived. But presently we stop; a man jumps from the box and fastens some enormous chains to the wheels, and then we start slowly down an almost up and down bit of street, turn sharply to the right, and find ourselves at the door of our hotel. No impression can be formed of where we are situated, and after dinner we retire, to wait for the morning light.

What a scene then lies before us! Sloping to the shore of Lake Leman is part of the pretty town. There lies the exquisite robin's-egg blue lake, dimpling in the morning sunshine, and beyond it, and down each shore as far as the eye can reach, are the mountains, some lying in deep

purple shadow, some crested with sparkling snow, and
some sweeping down to the lake an unbroken expanse of
green.   Here and there upon its lovely water floats a boat,
and we are so high above it that it looks like a tiny toy.
No more enchanting introduction could be made to Switzerland than this, and it is difficult to drag one's self away
from the view of lake and mountains even for a ramble
through the town.

All the streets are steep and narrow, and the only level
place in the town seems to be the square in front of the
cathedral.   This square is also the market place, and this
particular morning it was filled with temporary booths
and heaps and sacks of fruits and vegetables, while most
of the sellers were women, who kept up a constant chatter
among themselves.

The stores here in Lausanne are really attractive, the
people interesting, the gardens and buildings fine, and the
old Cathedral looming over it all seems to be the protector
of the little town.

In the cemetery lies John Kemble, the great actor, who
died here.   Near our hotel is the garden where Gibbon
spent some of his busiest hours at work upon his " Rise
and Fall of the Roman Empire."   The house where he
lived was close here, and this garden adjoined his home,
while a little summer house, commanding a view of the
glorious lake, was his favorite place for writing; and he
tells us that it was in this summer house, late at night,
that he finished the last page of this his life-work.

We left Lausanne for Ouchy by a short piece of cable
railway which leads through a long tunnel, over which are
streets and buildings.   Ouchy is really the port of Lausanne, and it was here we took the steamer for Geneva.
It was at Ouchy, while confined to the town by bad

weather, that Byron wrote his " Prisoner of Chillon." The house in which he wrote it—the Ancre Inn—is no longer in existence, or rather it was made over into a large hotel. It is said that Byron was only two days in writing this nearly perfect piece of English verse.

The steamboats on Lake Leman—or Lake Geneva, as one prefers—are essentially pleasure boats. The whole deck is open and covered with a canvas awning, while the small cabin is used as a lunch room.

Sailing across the lake we stop at Evian, which is a fashionable watering-place, due to its excellent mineral waters. Tradition has it that Byron was once nearly lost just off Evian, on the lake, a terrible storm having arisen while he was out in a small boat.

We next touched at Thonon, which is another delightful health resort, crossed the lake again to Nyon, where we saw the former home of Joseph Bonaparte, a handsome chateau, and then approached Coppet, where, commanding a rare view of the lake, stands the chateau of Madame de Stael and her father, M. Necker, the famous French minister. It is a large, plain building, having a tower at each end, and it was here, under the elevating influence of the eternal hills, that much of Madame de Stael's best work was done.

And now we approach Geneva, with its breakwater and lighthouse, its graceful bridges spanning the rivers Rhone and Arve, its magnificent buildings and background of snow-capped mountains. On the left as we sail to the quay, between the lower ranges of hills, looms Mt. Blanc. We know it is sixty miles away, but so grandly its white peaks show in the sunshine that it looks to be just on the other side of the hills.

Upon a nearer acquaintance with Geneva one ceases to

wonder why so many Americans and English contentedly settle down here for a year or two. It is so immaculately clean that it attracts one at once, and its streets are broad and lined with trees, which also adds to its beauty.

The great Rousseau was born in Geneva, and a little island, reached from one of the bridges, has his statue upon it. Here, too, came Calvin to live and preach, and after visiting his house, we went to the Cathedral, St. Pierre, where stands the pulpit and canopy as they did in Calvin's day.

Perhaps the most notable of the sights in Geneva, to an American, is the room in the Hotel de Ville where the Geneva award was signed. Here are framed photographs in groups of the eminent lawyers America sent over to look after the interests of her citizens. On a raised platform, as a much-prized ornament, rests a real Yankee plow, sent as a gift from Ohio. In this Hotel de Ville, or City Hall, is the ancient Barons' stairway, up which the barons used to ride to reach the council hall.

The museum is really a very enjoyable one and has some good pictures and statuary. It is named for its generous donor, General Rath, who left his fortune to establish it.

There is a very pretty Russian church that attracts most travellers, a beautiful theatre and conservatory of music, while most charming drives can be taken in almost any direction out of town.

The hydraulic machines for supplying the city with water are well worth a visit, and one can study the whole mechanism of the machines from a good-sized model of wood in the building.

Another of the sights at Geneva is the junction of the rivers Rhone and Arve. Just below the town, with a narrow strip of land between them, flow the bright blue Rhone and dark yellow waters of the Arve. The best view of the junction is obtained from a pretty garden that is within a pleasant drive of Geneva, and at the entrance of which one can obtain a delicious lemonade or cup of coffee. The garden is high upon the bank of the Rhone and from the walks one looks down upon the two rivers rushing to meet; and long after the waters ought to have mingled, they flow along together like a ribbon with one edge blue and one yellow.

On the road out to these gardens one passes the immense wine vaults built in the sides of the hill, where wine is stored. The openings are closed with enormous slabs of granite, and each is numbered and dated. Pretty pleasure gardens and cafes are met with here and there, and troops of merry people come and go between these and the city.

There is one feature of Geneva that attracts ladies, and that is the sealskin garments that can be bought for almost nothing in comparison to what we pay here at home.

The music boxes also are exceedingly fine, and Americans, they tell me, are their best customers. I saw the duplicate of one that ex-Governor Ames had brought home for his beautiful house, and it was wonderfully fine. Patti, also, had just bought one of the best they had, and I heard it play the overture to William Tell. It was like a grand organ and orchestra combined. The barrels were about five feet long, and each one had a separate musical selection. When a particular opera or overture was desired, that particular barrel was inserted. I noticed that she had selected for its performance a goodly number of Wagner's works.

Pretty jewelry abounds in Geneva, and wood carving as well.

But one could ramble on forever, on Geneva—and in it, too, for that matter—where one may idle away the hours of the day in walks, and drives, and boating, with silent hours of rest. watching the shadows creep over the mountains, and the glowing and fading of the sunlight on the crowned head of Mont Blanc, and where the evenings may be enjoyed in the pretty Kursaal Garden listening to the orchestra, the Kursaal Hall hearing a good concert, or wandering about to the different cafes where one may sip coffee and listen to selections of French opera and songs of the day.

CHAPTER II.

Leaving Geneva one bright July day, we again passed by Coppet and Nyon, on Lake Leman; but this time we went by rail, and the piece of road is over one of the most beautiful sections of country in Europe.

Being built along the sides of the vine-clad hills, we ride for miles aniong the vineyards, which are so close to the railway tracks that one could almost reach from the cars and pick the grapes.

Far down the sweep of the hills lie quaint villages, with buildings looking for all the world like the copies we used to follow in our drawing-books at school. Across the brilliant blue lake, from the other shore rise the rugged, snow-capped Alps, with Mt. Blanc towering over all.

As the sun rises higher and higher and its heat begins to be felt, from all the lower peaks stream threads of water from the melting snow. We watch them as they gather force from height and other mingling streams, and finally see them shoot over some projecting bowlder and fall, a glittering shower, into the lake.

The light and shade on the mountains, the soft summer haze, the snow, so brilliant in the sunlight, together with the glorious expanse of lake, and nearer view of gorge, deep valley, vineyards and picturesque towns, make up this marvellous view. One seems to have arrived at a plane above this world of ours, and to be looking back upon its beauty and sweetness, just as one looks back upon happy years from the plane of a prosaic life.

From Lausanne we go to Berne by way of Freyburg, and have a very good view of this strikingly picturesque town. The suspension bridge across the valley is one of the finest in the world. The bridge is supported on four cables, each cable having about 1,050 wires. The cables are then run into the ground some distance at each end of the bridge, and are then carried down some shafts cut in the solid rock, the shafts are filled with masonry, and the ends of the cables, coming still from the shafts, are fastened to huge blocks of stone. It is said that Switzerland supplied all the materials for this bridge; that the iron came from Berne, the masonry from the quarries in the Jura and the woodwork from the forests around Freyburg.

Freyburg is built upon the high bank of the winding Saane River, and the old wall and battlements about it make it interesting and peculiar.

At Berne we make a stop, for there is much to see in this old town that was founded in the year 1191. As you all know, the meaning of the word Berne is *bear;* but perhaps you do not remember that the founder of the town killed a bear upon this site, and named it so on account of this event.

One of the sights in the town is the bear-pit, where some poor specimens are confined. Large numbers used to be kept at the expense of the city; but when the French got into Berne, they carried off all the bears to Paris, and put them in the Jardin des Plantes. However, after peace was declared, the bears were again made—one might almost say—household gods. All the fountains,

signs and public buildings have a bear of some sort upon
them, and the armorial badge of the town is the bear.

The high bridge over the river Aar is one of the sights
of interest in Berne; it is ninety-three feet high, and
from it one obtains a very pretty view of the city. The
buildings are nearly all constructed with heavy arcades,
but these are lower than in most other cities in Europe,
and consequently the stores are very dark, and are not so
attractive to strangers.

There are numerous fountains about the streets, and
from these the people are constantly carrying water. Some
of these fountains are very odd. One in particular represents a hideous ogre, who is eating children, and doing it
with a relish, too. It is said that the mothers in Berne
frighten their disobedient children with this realistic
figure, and threaten them with being taken and devoured
by this same monster.

One day when I was in Berne there was a fete, and all
the fountains and buildings were draped with bunting, and
wreaths and flags were flying from every available spot.
Directly opposite our carriages — we were a party of
Americans — we caught sight of the American flag, flung
to the breeze from the window of the American consul at
Berne. It would have done your heart good to hear the
shout of greeting we gave it. We waved our handker-
chiefs; the gentlemen took off their hats and waved them;
we gave three cheers, and then three more. One can form
no conception of the joyful and proud swelling of heart
with which one views the dear old flag when coming upon
it in a foreign city and country. The people on the streets
stopped and watched us with smiles of sympathy, for the
Swiss are eminently patriotic. They took in the situation
at a glance, and showed no surprise. It is a fact, however,

that to the European nothing is surprising that an American does. We have the reputation of being a most eccentric people, and long ago they gave up, over there, expecting us to do as they do. But they like us, as a whole people, and to the common people of Europe our country seems like a land where gold grows in the streets, and one has only to stoop, and gather it.

The cathedral is a fine specimen of fifteenth century architecture, and has a grand organ which is played each day at 6.30 P.M ; so that for a franc one may hear a good concert whenever in the mood for it.

The cathedral terrace is the place in Berne for the view.

It is built upon a wall of solid masonry, over a hundred feet above the bank of the Aar, has a high parapet, pretty trees, walks, and seats, some booths, where Swiss wood carvings are sold, and a handsome bronze statue of the founder of the city, who killed the bear, Berthold V., of some unpronounceable Swiss place.

Below this terrace, directly under the wall, there are one or two old streets with houses so quaint and foreign that they delight the eye   By these streets flows the river, and here upon the banks are the women and children busily at work with the washing, kneeling beside the flat bit of plank or stone, while with a flat wooden sort of paddle they slap and bang the garments, occasionally dipping them into the water, and again scooping up some water upon them by means of the paddle or their hands.

The view from this terrace is unrivalled. The whole range of the Bernese Alps lies spread out before us, and by the purple depths or faint haze between the snow mountains, one can judge of the immense distances that lie between them, and the deep valleys and depressions that separate them. Between this outer wall of snow peaks and us lie range upon range of lofty green mountains and rolling, undulating hills, and over these the sun is shining, bringing out all the delicate tints of green and brown that only nature can paint.

We see the Wetterhorn, like a marble mountain in the blue distance ; while in the nearer range lies the Niesen, barren and lonely, and nearer yet, the lower green range of hills.

But the chief object of interest in Berne is the clock tower, which stands very nearly in the centre of the town, and where four of the principal streets cross each other. It was built by this same Berthold V.—who killed the bear—in the year 1100 and something, and was at that time part of the outer wall of the city. Five minutes before the hour is to strike, people begin to collect in front of the tower to watch the puppets work. It is best to see it when it is going to strike a number of times.

Three minutes before the hour a wooden cock at one side of the clock flaps his wings and gives a lusty crow ; then we wait one minute more, when, on the opposite side of the clock, where there is an image of an old man sitting, out comes a small procession of bears, and these walk around the old man ; then the cock gives another crow, and we hold our breath and try to look all over the tower at once, for fear we will miss some part of the show. And now, on the top of the tower, a fool, in cap and bells, strikes a large bell with a hammer. The strokes of this hammer are counted by the old man, who turns an hourglass, raises a sceptre he holds in his other hand, and while doing all this he also opens his mouth. There is another bear, that, at the same time, bows his head. As a wind-up to the performance the cock crows again.

It is great fun, not only to watch the clock, but to

watch the people in their eagerness to see it all, for they keep calling out to each other to watch this or that figure, and for the first comer it is rather bewildering to grasp it all.

One feels well repaid for having seen Berne, and finds the short railway journey to the Lake of Thun very pleasant. Passing Thun station, the boat is taken at Scherzligen, which is the railway terminus on the shore of the lake.

The boats are exactly like those on Lake Leman, and one prepares for an hour and a half of keen delight on this lovely sheet of water. The lake is about eleven miles long and two wide, and near the town of Thun the hills that rise from it are covered with vineyards, villas and woods of pine and oak. Some of the villas are very handsome, and are owned by titled and wealthy people, who come to this quiet spot to enjoy a few months' rest from the busy cares of society.

As we go further down the lake the mountains on the left become rugged and grand, and we see sheer precipices hundreds of feet high. On one of these mountains we see a small cascade leaping down toward the lake, and just above it there is the Cave of St. Beatus. This holy man, so the story goes, came over from Britain to convert the Helvetians to Christianity, and looking about for some convenient spot in the mountains where he might make a hermitage for himself, he espied this cave. Unfortunately, it was already occupied by a dragon, but St. Beatus ordered him from the cave, and so great was the power of this holy man, the order was immediately obeyed. The legend has it, also, that the saint always crossed the lake upon his cloak, which, spread upon the waters, bore him in safety across.

The boat stops at the several landings where there are tiny villages and hotels, and finally brings us to Darligen, where we take an observation car on the railway, and in five minutes find ourselves at Interlaken.

It is impossible to tell wherein lies the charm that all people find in Interlaken. The little town is built along one main street, and is made up almost entirely of hotels and stores. By hotels, of course, I mean the lodging house and the " pension " as well, together with the restaurants that must go with these.

The best hotel, both for comfort and location, is, I think, the Beau Rivage, for it lies at the end of the town just by the pretty bridge that crosses the river Aar, while back of it runs the river, and from the bank rises a wooded mountain, while at its base and close to the river runs the same little piece of railway that brought us from Darligen. In front of the house there is a beautiful garden, with trees and fountains, and all about are little tables and comfortable seats and chairs. One may breakfast or lunch here, *al fresco*, spend a whole day with a book from the library—just off the drawing-room—or sit in the evening shadows and listen to bands of singers from Naples or from the Swiss villages among the mountains.

From the windows and the garden, rising between two beautiful wooded mountains, we see the wonderful Jungfrau. It is twenty miles away, but in its white purity, rising against the bright blue sky, it looks to be not half a mile from us. Every hour of the day it changes its color as the sun strikes across its glittering snows, and the enormous glaciers throw deeper and deeper shadows as the day wears late. At night, when the sun has set and the little town is nearly dark, we sit and watch the wonderful light that glows upon this " young maiden," for we are so shut in by the mountains that the sun cannot reach us, but can still throw its last lingering rays up to the white breast of the Jungfrau. It flushes from orange to deep red, then fades to palest pink, and finally dies away in tints of tender gray that fall into dark shadow. And so she sleeps, till the next glad morning with its first sunbeams touches her to vivid life again.

CHAPTER III.

There is no spot in Switzerland more convenient for enjoyable excursions than Interlaken. One of the most
thoroughly delightful ones is to go over the mountains to
the village of Lauterbrunnen, to visit the Staubbach Falls.
We leave Interlaken in the morning by carriage, and
shortly roll through the streets of a typical Swiss village.

The houses are built with the long, sloping roof that
overhangs a sort of balcony, and under the eaves of this
roof are hanging to dry bunches of corn and the family
linen. Upon the roof are laid rows of huge stones, to
hold it down when the terrific winds sweep through the
valley.

Upon the fronts of many of the houses are statements
as to the age of the house, the builder, and often a text,
and these have the letters carved in the wood.

The arrangement of the Swiss house is peculiar. The
lower portion is reserved for the cattle, the middle for the
family, and under the roof is stored the food for both the
family and the cattle.

The road to Lauterbrunnen follows the winding of the
Lütschine River, a rushing, foaming stream, and this leads
up till we reach a sort of plateau, from which the view

of the mountains and the two valleys of the river is some thing grand. The river is here divided by a sort of tongue of land, and the two branches of the stream are called the Black and the White Lütschine, from the muddy, discolored waters of the one and the clear, transparent waters of the other.

Here and there along the road are peasants with the long Alpine horn, and tossing to them a few small coins, we are repaid by hearing the long, musical notes from the horn echo and re-echo from cliffs and mountains till the whole air seems full of music.

Little children and women run along beside the carriage and offer for sale luscious plums and the pretty hand-made lace for which the women in this section of Switzerland are noted. The prices are moderate, and there is nothing unpleasant in the manner of offering it to a possible purchaser.

As we wind along by the river, on our right rise wooded mountains, with here and there places where the heavy snows of winter have torn a wide path down the sheer sides, taking in their train trees and rocks, and down these paths will come dashing streams from the melting snows on the summits; and among the broken and scattered rocks tender ferns and bright green mosses, together with delicate wild flowers, are courageously growing.

Across the river the mountains rise in shapes like vast cathedrals and castles, and before us rise the Silberhorn and the Jungfrau, covered with perpetual snows.

The little hamlet of Lauterbrunnen lies in a green valley surrounded with mountains, some heavily wooded, some grass grown, others of bare ragged rock crowned with snow, and the white majestic Silberhorn ever keeping its silent watch.

The little inn at which we put up the horses is a busy place, for it is the rendezvous for all the parties that come here to visit the Falls. Parties for a mountain climb are ready to set forth, each clad in true regulation rig, stout boots, heavily nailed, short skirts for ladies, short trousers for gentlemen, wide hats, with bunches of wild flowers on the side, and the Alpen stock. A troop of merry people, mounted on sturdy mountain horses, are bidding last good-bys to some friends, and we hear that they are going up to Mürren for the view, and will return later and take their carriages back to Interlaken.

All about, on the sides of the hills, are the chalets of the peasants, the whole population of the little village being about 1400. The chief industries are wood-carving and lace-making.

During the long, cruel winter, while they are shut into their valley by snow and ice, they work busily for the large dealers in these goods at Berne, Lucerne, Geneva and Interlaken. The wood carvings are exquisite, and one cannot fail to wonder where these lonely people get the knowledge for this remarkable work. The trade is handed down from father to son, and the results they obtain are marvellous. The most intricate and perfect piece of work they accomplish is a reproduction of the Swiss chalet. Even to the most minute detail it is perfect. It is then fitted with a music-box attachment, and also with a complete wine set, in pretty glass. The roof lifts for finding the wine set, but the music-box is hidden in the lower part of the house.

Another very novel arrangement which they make is a chair that has under the seat a music-box, so that when one sits in it the machinery starts and one hears the strains of some familiar opera.

All around the valley where Lauterbrunnen lies tiny streams of water are falling from the summits of the mountains. I counted one day thirty of such fine silver threads, for there had been snow on the tops for some days, and a hot sun had come out and the snow was rapidly disappearing.

But the fall we had come to see was the Staubbach, or " Dust Stream," that falls from a height of 900 feet. It is so slender a stream and hits a projecting surface of the cliff at such an angle that it is thrown into a delicate spray that looks like lace, or golden dust, as the sun happens to strike it. At times as the wind blows it, it looks like long, streaming white hair. It is said that when the clouds are low and settle down upon the summits of the mountains that the Staubbach Falls seem to spring from the very clouds themselves.

We walked up the tiny, winding path through the field that brings us to the foot of the Falls, and sat for an hour watching the different forms the stream took and the rainbow tints as the sun shone upon it.

At the entrance to the path a boy was stationed with a small cannon, which for a few centimes he would fire, that we might hear the wonderful echo.

The piece of road leading from the inn up to the Falls has along one side a row of tiny shops where lace, woodcarvings and odds and ends made from horn and agate are sold. Back of one shop the man keeps some pretty, graceful chamois, and near another a young fellow has four or five magnificent St. Bernard dogs.

The drive back to Interlaken was full of interest and enjoyment, for every aspect of the mountains is delightful. One very curious combination of gigantic mountain peaks along our route makes a nearly perfect thumb and four fingers.

Having an extra day in Interlaken to dispose of, various members of our party decided to spend it in various ways.

Some went to visit the wonderful Grindelwald glaciers ; some made an ascent of one of the high mountains ; some made it a complete day of rest and spent the whole time in the garden among the flowers and fountains with that most excellent of all companions, a good book ; while some of us took a long walk through two little villages and a ramble in the beautiful wooded slopes on the bank of the river.

Near one of these villages we came across the funniest sight I think it was ever my fortune to see. Not far from a small farmhouse was a fenced-in family graveyard, with a most imposing monument. The family had evidently been preparing the regular supply of enormous sausages for the winter, for all along the fence and hanging in festoons across the monument were strings upon strings of them drying in the sun.

In the evening it is very gay in Interlaken, and strains of music greet one at every turn. Bands of singers from the mountains come down to the hotels and give concerts, in which the real " Yodel " is heard to perfection. These peasants wear the true Swiss costume, that is so fast disappearing, and the women are very smart, with their enormous starched sleeves, black bodices and silver chains pendant from the shoulders.

The voices are strident and coarse, but the novelty of the music lends it a certain charm.

But when a little band of singers from Naples stroll up the quiet street, dressed in bright and glowing colors, and each with a mandolin or guitar, we are all in a flutter of excitement, for the setting of this music is just right, the soft and tender summer night, the faint, sweet odor of flowers and trees, the far-off glimmering stars, and in the trembling light we catch the glint of dark, passionate eyes and gleaming teeth.

And now comes a musical little prelude, and a clear, fine tenor voice begins the refrain of " Funiculi, Funicula," and presently the merry chorus strikes in " Tra la, la, la," and as our pulses beat in unison with the jolly music, there comes the peculiar little *snap* we all know so well, and the brilliant electric lights flash and turn the whole scene into fairyland. With one of these companies of Italian singers is a blind girl, who plays and sings well.

Near the hotel there is an open-air theatre and concert hall, and every evening there is a lively performance and concert of some sort.

Not far down the street, and in the heart of the little town, is the Kursaal, where a superior orchestra is engaged every season. A large music stand, the top of which forms an immense sounding-board, is built in the beautiful garden, while in the gravel walks are innumerable small tables, with chairs, where people sit for the entire evening, drink beer and listen to the music. The Kursaal itself has a large reading-room well supplied with papers, a refreshment-room and grand dance hall, together with a room where games of chance are going on all the evening, and where a person may lose or win four or five francs during that time.

And so the time goes in quiet Interlaken, and one bright, sunshiny morning we wake to find our stay here at an end, and we betake ourselves and our belongings to the small railway again, *en route* for Lucerne.

CHAPTER IV.

THE BRUNIG PASS—LUNGERN SEE—ROTZBERG—OLD
BRIDGES—MUSIC OF THE ORGAN—THOR-
WALDSEN'S LION—ASCENT OF THE
RHIGI—CLOUD EFFECTS.

From Interlaken to Bonigen, where we take the little
steamer on the Lake of Brienz, is only a few moments
ride by rail, in observation cars. The lake is beautiful,
with its setting of wooded mountains, is about nine miles
long and two wide, and has a depth, in some portions,
of 2,000 feet, while its average depth is 500 feet.

Just before we strike across the lake to the town of
Brienz we touch at the Giessbach landing, and watch the
passengers take the cars on the little mountain railway for
the hotel. Shortly after leaving the landing we pass the
famous Giessbach Falls and have a most excellent view of
them. These falls are unique, and look more like an
artificial waterfall than one formed by nature. They come
leaping down the side of the mountain over what seem to
be terraces, and are closely shut in by the rich green fir
trees and tangle of underbrush and ferns, till they reach
the shore of the lake, when they tumble in silvery beauty
into the blue depths.

Giessbach is a popular resort for travellers, and one of
the chief attractions here is the illumination of the falls
each evening during the season. The effect of the colored
lights on the sparkling steam is magical.

Crossing the lake, we land at Brienz, and at once take the cars for the trip over the Brunig Pass. For the first three miles the road is comparatively level, then at the foot of the mountains we stop at a station where, after much backing and side-tracking, the train is divided into sections, with an engine for each, and, with a start of perhaps five minutes between each train, we begin the ascent of the Pass. As we climb up and up the scene below us broadens, until the whole wide valley of the Aar lies smiling in the sunshine, with its background of snow mountains and gleaming waterfalls.

All the way up the Pass, in the most impossible looking spots, we find the small houses of the hardy Swiss peasant, and are sure to discover that he has chosen a level plateau—however small—and that it has a southern exposure, where every ray of the sun may be a benefit.

On the summit of the Pass we have lunch, and then in the same detached cars begin to crawl down the other side of the mountains. And here a new view presents itself. We look down upon the valley of Sarnen, with grim Mount Pilatus as a background, and in the near distance see the pretty Lungern See—in reality a small lake. This was once a large sheet of water, but the peasants in the neighborhood, desiring to acquire extra lands for cultivation, fifty odd years ago tapped this lake and let off the water, till they had reduced it to one-half its size. It is said that it involved a labor of 19,000 days, and that it was performed by the peasants. The gain was five hundred acres of excellent land.

Gyswyl, one of the little towns we next pass, has quite a history. Two hundred years ago the torrent Lauibach brought such a mass of timber, rock and general refuse into the valley that the river Aar became dammed, and half the village was swept away. The pent-up waters of the river made a large lake that lasted for one hundred and thirty years. This lake was finally let into the Lake of Sarnen by means of an artificial canal.

And now on the left lies the Lake of Sarnen, a truly beautiful sheet of water, and skirting its shore we presently reach the town of the same name, the capital of one of the divisions of a canton, and the seat of government.

The character of the scenery about here is entirely different from that we have been seeing. The mountains have dropped to gently swelling hills, upon whose sides are vast orchards and gardens, and the whole valley presents an appearance of quiet thrift and harmony.

There is nothing striking in the scenery between here and Alpnach-am-Gstaad, when we take the boat for Lucerne. We are really on Alpnach Lake, shut in by hills and mountains, with giant Pilatus looming on our left, his head lost in the clouds.

Passing through a narrow strait and through a bridge that extends from the village of Stanzstad to the opposite shore, we see the picturesque watch tower that is five hundred years old. The story of this tower is that a boat loaded with Austrian partisans was swamped by having hurled into it from this same tower an enormous stone.

I neglected to say that on the shore of Alpnach Lake is the castle of Rotzberg, which was the first stronghold of the Austrians that the Swiss got possession of. Of course a woman had a finger in this pie — as usual. One of the young servants in the castle had a Swiss lover, who occasionally visited her by means of a rope ladder. By this same convenient means of transit he introduced a number of his companions, who easily surprised and overpowered the garrison.

And now the lake broadens, and again the mountains reach high toward heaven, and sweeping around a bend past Kramerstein and Stutz we reach Lucerne.

The view of Lucerne from the lake is strikingly beautiful. Along its lake front extends a broad promenade shaded by handsome horsechestnut trees; along this are built imposing hotels and the fine Kursaal. Back of the city there is a part of the ancient wall, with some of the watch towers in good preservation.

The city is divided by the river Reuss, and a wide handsome modern bridge leads from the railway station to the chief side of the city. Other bridges cross the river, two of which are very old and curious. The lower one, nearest the station, is called the Kapell Bridge, and from the timbers that support the roof seventy-seven paintings on wood are suspended. They represent scenes in the lives of the two patron saints of Lucerne — St. Leger and St. Maurice — and scenes from Swiss history. In going from the right to the left shore the pictures are those of the saints, while in going in the opposite direction those of the history are seen.

Close to this bridge is the old watch tower that once was used as a lighthouse, and which gave the name to Lucerne — "Lucerna." Still another old bridge, and far more famous than the Kapell, has paintings representing the "Dance of Death."

The church — St. Leger — is one of the most interesting in Europe. It has regular seats, and the wood-work is so old it is full of holes and perforations. The organ is arranged with reference to the effects that can be produced with such an instrument.

Every evening at 6.30 there is a concert, and words fail me to describe the delicious harmonics and melodies that thrill the very air about one during this hour. The *vox humana* stop in the organ is marvellous, and one can scarcely believe it is not a human voice that rises and falls with the flood of harmony. Suddenly there comes a sound of distant thunder, but it is swallowed up in a grand religious chant that has caught up the one wonderful voice. But in a moment it comes again, nearer than before, but through it all the chant goes on. Then comes a sound of rushing wind through great trees, and the branches bend, and sway, and sweep together, and a terrific crash of thunder shakes the very stones under our feet. Down comes the rain, first in great splashes, then in hurrying drops, and then in a down-pour, and occasionally, through it all, one catches a strain of the solemn chant. Then the storm begins to subside, and we hear the roll of the thunder far beyond the hills. The rain ceases; birds begin to twitter and sing; the leaves shake off their clinging drops; afar up the hillside we hear the tinkling of sheep-bells; and from the great organ comes swelling forth the full harmonies of an anthem, while high above it all sings the one pure, clear voice, as if coming out of heaven itself.

Was it all a dream?

Through the open doors the soft evening light comes stealing in. A rustle and deep murmur of pleasure all about us brings back the present and the reality of what we have heard.

Yes, it was all the organ. The voice, the chanting, the thunder and storm, the song of birds and branches. Listening to such music the soul rises above petty worldly cares and disappointments, and for a time at least, we walk with the angels.

The chief attraction in Lucerne is the monument to the

Swiss guard who fell while defending the Tuilleries at
Paris in the first revolution.   When friends and servants
deserted Louie XVI. and Marie Antoinette, the Swiss
guard remained faithful, and fought like tigers to protect
them, and when that failed, to cover their escape.   The
design of the monument is by Thorwaldsen, and the work
was done by a sculptor from Constance, Ahorn by name.
It represents a colossal lion who is dying from a spear
wound in the side—the spear is broken in the wound.   In
spite of the death agony he is suffering, he is trying to
protect a shield upon which are engraved the fleur-de-lis
of the Bourbons, which shield he holds in his paws.   The
lion is carved in the side of the solid rock, is twenty-
eight feet long and eighteen feet high.   Below the lion
are carved the names of the officers who fell during
this terrible time.   All about the face of the monument
are growing mosses, ferns and creeping vines, and in front
of it a large basin receives the clear water that flows down
beside the cliff from springs higher up.   One of the most
beautiful things that T. B. Aldrich has given us has this
monument to point its moral :—

> " We ask fair wind and favorable tide;
>   From the dead Danish sculptor let us learn
>   To make occasion, not to be denied.
>   Against the sheer, precipitous mountain side
>   Thorwaldsen carved his lion at Lucerne."

Seats to accommodate the visitors are placed in front
of the monument, and many persons sit for hours and
study this grand conception of strength, valor and faith-
fulness.

Near here is what is called the Glacier Garden, and one
can see the effect of the marvellous action of the glaciers
in the circular wells, or holes, produced by a constant
rotary motion.

The ascent of the Rhigi is an excursion that all visitors
at Lucerne make. The boat leaves for Vitznau several
times a day, and the sail is very pleasant. Shortly
after leaving the pier we pass on the left a high sort of
promontory, upon which is a fine chateau, and just here
opens up another arm of the lake, called Kussnacht, while
on the right opens Alpnach Bay, by which we came to
Lucerne.

Arriving at Vitznau, we enter the cars for the trip up
the Rhigi, and find them open upon all sides, with the seats
going across, like an open horsecar. The journey up is
much more comfortable than upon the Mount Washington
railway, and one does not have that disagreeable sensation
of being choked by the angle at which one's head is kept.
Each car has a locomotive, and these are not connected in
any way, so that in case of accident to the engine the pas-
senger car would not be dragged from the track, but would
hold by its own brakes. Coming down it rests against the
engine, and going up the engine pushes it.

I wish space allowed for a description of this railway, the
engines, and the ingenious contrivance of the brakes, but
it would make a chapter in itself.

One of the strange things about the ascent of the Rhigi
is that at short intervals the train stops at various large
hotels, built upon the level plateaux, and from one of them
a branch road leads off around and down the mountain on
another side.

At one place the railway crosses a bridge, so frail and
so high above the horrible gorge below that one holds the
breath till the solid earth is again under the tracks.

The kulm, or summit, of the Rhigi has no trees, but there
is green turf, and until the absolute summit is reached
there are masses of tiny bluebells growing everywhere.

A large hotel is found here. with handsome parlors and dining-rooms. and during the whole season the house is crowded with guests each night. Who come up on the chance of seeing the sun rise.

Back of the hotel there is a still higher point to be reached on the mountain, and here are found numberless dealers in small articles of Swiss manufacture, who generally do a good business with the tourists. for each person wishes to carry home a souvenir of the trip up among the clouds.

It is a rare occurrence to have a good day for the view. for mist and clouds are nearly always hanging over the Rhigi. A day when the clouds are sweeping over it and rolling off is the best time to really enjoy the view. For the fleeting glimpses of the whole Bernese Alps are so grand—the Lake of the Four Cantons. in shape like a cross; the blue Lake of Zug; Pilatus, dark and grim; and the valleys and villages below.

The cloud effects are wonderful. Sometimes they will come rolling up about the summit like gigantic waves that swallow us up in mist and rain; in half an hour all is commotion again. and the wind will tear and rend the clouds till they are masses of shreds and tangled odds and ends; and while this is going on the sun will come out and all around us are bits of rainbow and clouds of rose and violet.

Then these melt away. the sun grows clearer. and far below lies the beautiful picture we saw before.

High above the world you may look down upon its material beauties, and study nature in all her grandeur and majesty.

CHAPTER V.

In coming down the Rhigi we experience that peculiar
sensation that the lakes and villages are coming up to
meet us. People who make balloon ascents speak of this
feeling when coming down, and it is strikingly noticed in
the descent of the Eiffel Tower at Paris.

Taking the boat again at Vitznau, on the lake, we pass
between two rocky headlands, one a projection of the Rhigi
and the other of the Burgenstock, and known as the
" Noses."

It seems to us that we have reached the end of the lake
but presently we sail into a large oval-shaped lake, or
rather, as it is called, the Gulf of Buochs. Buochs is a
pretty village on the shore from which it takes its name.

On the opposite shore is Gersau, which has a most
peculiar history. It occupies perhaps a space of three
miles long by two wide, and is almost wholly on the slope
of the mountains. For four hundred years this little spot
was an independent state, having perhaps 2000 inhabi-
tants. The people bought their freedom from the lords
of Lucerne, whose serfs they had been till then. It took
them ten years to collect the necessary sum, which history

says was 690 pounds of pfenniges. This freedom was bought in 1390, and they governed themselves, electing a governor and council till the year 1798.

One fact is worthy of mention in regard to the public policy of Gersau during these years. Although they had a strict criminal jurisdiction of their own, and a public gallows, not a single execution took place during these four hundred years.

Gersau is so sheltered by mountains and the sun shines upon it so warmly that it is called the Nice of Switzerland, and many persons spend the winter in its pleasant hotel. Passing around the promontory of Trieb the boat crosses the lake to Brunnen, and here opens the beautiful bay of Uri, one of the most beautiful in Switzerland.

Brunnen was once of great importance commercially, and was the place with which all Italian business was carried on. Its position is fine, commanding both branches of the lake and the extended mountain ranges.

The Bay of Uri, or Bay of Fluelen—whichever one wishes to call it—is like none other in Switzerland. The mountains rise from its waters in sheer precipices, and are most wild and imposing. The lake is said to be over 1100 feet deep.

Just across from Brunnen there is a peculiar slab-like stone projecting from the lake, at the foot of the precipice, and upon this is carved a tribute to Schiller, who so graphically and beautifully has told the story of William Tell. Here we are in the midst of the scenes where, according to tradition, Tell lived and fought for his beloved Switzerland.

Just beyond the Schiller rock, the precipice drops a little; some earth has fallen from above, in which some fine trees have taken root and flourished, and near these is a small green spot, which history points out as the rendez-vous of the three founders of Swiss liberty and freedom. They met at dead of night in this isolated spot, in the fourteenth century, and so carefully and perfectly were their plans laid and executed that their country was freed from the hated Austrian rule.

Upon this green spot the tourist is invited to drink of three springs that miraculously sprang up upon this meet-ing-place; and one drinks to the memory of these hardy and patriotic sons of the mountains both with admiration and respect.

On the opposite shore, at the foot of the Axenberg, on the margin of the lake, is Tell's Chapel. Upon this spot, according to the story, Tell jumped ashore from the boat in which Gessler was taking him a prisoner, to Kussnacht —up nearer Lucerne.

The chapel is nothing but a sort of open arcade, lined with the commonest and rudest sort of pictures, repre-senting historical scenes in the freeing of Switzerland. Once each year mass is said in this chapel, and boats bring people from every part of the lake to do honor to the memory of William Tell.

In this prosaic nineteenth century they are slowly, but surely, smashing the idols of our past veneration. Chris-topher Columbus is painted for us as one who was " up to snuff," and having found out from the Icelanders that there was a promised land over here, came and discovered it; Pocahontas never risked her head for John Smith; a man in Venice told me this very summer that Othello was no Moor, but that his name was " Othello More"; and they tell us that such a man as Tell never performed the feats of valor we have loved him for. The nineteenth century is all right, but a line must be drawn somewhere;

and amidst the scenes of Swiss history, and seeing the devotion of a whole people to even a myth—if it be one —let us hold fast to the myth with them, and offer freely our own sympathy and admiration.

From here to Fluelen, at the southern extremity of the lake, is only a short distance, and then we return to Lucerne.

No pleasanter place to pass an evening can be found than the Kursaal at Lucerne, and visitors from all the hotels stroll in here during the evening to hear the music and eat ices. A pretty theatre forms part of the establishment, and during the summer light operas and popular plays are presented.

And now the time has come when we must say adieu to Lucerne and the glorious mountains we have learned to love so well, so we take the train one pleasant morning en route for Bâle.

Our last glimpse of Lucerne is something to always remember. We cross the rushing river Reuss as it flows from the Lake of Lucerne, spin across the river Emme, and looking back, see Lucerne lying along the lake with a background of glittering snow-crowned mountains, and between us and the city the undulating line of battlemented wall, with the old watch-towers rising here and there above it.

Soon upon our sight appears the beautiful blue Lake of Sempach, and it was near these shores that a memorable battle for Swiss independence took place. One of the most heroic deeds of valor that history has left us was here performed by one of the Swiss knights. The Austrians had nearly routed the Swiss troops, and were pressing them back to defeat with their advancing spears. With a cry to his countrymen to remember his wife and little ones, Arnold of Winkelried sprang to the front and gathered into his opened arms all the spears he could grasp, forcing them into his bosom. The surprise and the break this made in the Austrian rank gave the Swiss the one opportunity they needed, and they rushed upon their foe, who, loaded with armor, were no match for the swift and hardy Swiss when once the solid opposing ranks were broken. Hundreds of the Austrians were killed, and each year anniversary masses are said for the repose of the souls of those who perished in this battle.

Olten, the railway junction of several lines, is rather a pretty town, nestling in the valley of the Jura.

There is, in all these towns, an air of thrift and prosperity that is very attractive to a New Englander. The spirit that urged them on to free their country from oppression and cruelty urges them to an individual independence, that shows itself in each farm and in each village.

As we approach Bâle through the valley of the Rhine, we pass another historical spot, where a small band of Swiss soldiers met and fought a superior number of French troops under the Dauphin—afterward Louis XI. This was called the battle of St. Jacob, and was to Switzerland what Thermopylæ was to Greece. The Swiss fought so bravely, and showed such determination and valor, that the French saw how advantageous it would be to gain them as allies, rather than to have such sturdy foes upon their own border.

The section of country around this battlefield has numerous vineyards that bear a grape which produces a very red wine, called "Schweizer Blut," literally "Swiss Blood."

The railway crosses a graceful bridge, and we find ourselves at Bâle, at the busy, bustling station. It is here

we make our first acquaintance with the river Rhine, which
divides Bâle, making two sections of the town—Great and
Little Bâle. On one side stretch the hills of the Black
Forest, and on the other the majestic range of the Jura,
while the " Blue Rhine sweeps along," and winds away
into the distance.

The cathedral is, of course, the chief object of interest.
It was begun in the tenth century, but was mostly rebuilt
during the fifteenth century, after an earthquake had
nearly destroyed it. Many famous people are buried in
the crypt, and in the chapter house, which one reaches
from the choir, are preserved the only remaining frescoes
of the original " Dance of Death," that was painted on the
walls of the Dominican church in Bâle in 1400 and something, as a remembrance of the plague. I believe it is not
known who painted these frescoes, although some authori-
ties say Holbein did them. But as they were in existance
fifty years before he was born, this opinion does not count
for much.

Holbein lived some six years in Bâle, and they were
years of hardship and poverty, which last drove him to the
painting of houses as a means of support. England seemed
to offer a prospect of success for him, and he removed
there, to meet fortune and fame. In the museum at Bâle
—which, by the way, has many valuable pictures and an
excellent collection of bronzes and coins—there are many
of Holbein's best works, and quite a number of his original
drawings.

The people of Bâle have an intense pride in their city,
and gifts for public purposes are constantly being made.
The population counts among its number many persons of
wealth and standing, and it is quite an aristocratic centre.

Till nearly the year 1800 the clocks in Bâle were kept

an hour ahead of those in all other Swiss towns. An old tradition said that the city was once saved from a terrible surprise, owing to the failure of a conspiracy. This conspiracy was that the gates should be opened to the enemy as the clocks struck twelve at midnight, but, in some miraculous way, the clocks struck *one* instead of twelve, and so the signal failed.

Our ten days in Switzerland are gone by, but they have been days full of profit and delight, and the memory of them will linger with us while life lasts. The mystery and majesty of the everlasting hills brings us into closer communion with Nature's God. We learn patience from the study of the lonely peaks lifting their gray and pallid faces ever toward the sky; we learn to look for the bright and sunny side of life as we wait and watch for the sun to touch the snows into rose and gold; we lose the worldly fever and unrest that hurries us through life as we allow the quiet influence of the grand stillness to steal into our hearts.

We say farewell to Switzerland, and as we look back longingly for a last glimpse of its beauties, a soft mist seems to arise that shuts out the fair picture; and turning toward Germany, as one turns from a deep pleasure of life to new experience and hope, lo! a tear falls.

One may shed tears of regret, and still they may be happy tears, and surely the remembrance of these ten days in Switzerland will be any other thing than a *sad* regret.

www.ingramcontent.com/pod-product-compliance
Lightning Source LLC
Chambersburg PA
CBHW021451090426
42739CB00009B/1712